HIS NAME IS NITHYANANDA

- Glimpses of an unfolding saga of bliss on planet Earth

PUBLISHED BY NITHYANANDA VEDIC SCIENCES UNIVERSITY PRESS
A division of Nithyananda Vedic Sciences University, USA

PREFACE

The ultimate quest of man, whatever may be his outer world seeking, is the quest for inner bliss. He seeks fulfillment at the being level. When he recognizes this quest, he is ready to take the leap towards his own enlightenment. The East has produced thousands of enlightened beings who have guided the rest of humanity through the same path.

Paramahamsa Nithyananda is a recognized enlightened master today. Born amidst rich spiritual heritage, and with a natural passion for the Truth, he experimented with yoga, integration of mind-body-spirit, meditation, tantra, vedanta and other Eastern metaphysical sciences, from the tender age of 3. He researched with thousands of inner science techniques before attaining enlightenment.

Single mindedly achieving his goal of enlightenment, today he is an awe-inspiring personality to millions of people around the world. He offers to every individual, instant clarity, spiritual wisdom, life solutions through meditation programs and the confidence to achieve. To the youth of today, he shows the tremendous possibility to experiment with oneself and achieve.

Paramahamsa Nithyananda set up his mission to help individuals raise themselves and connect with their higher self. He is on a mission to re-establish the science of inner bliss on planet Earth. He helps people actualize their inherent potential and transform into enlightened beings. He says, 'We need to create an enlightened society that lives with a strong conviction about the Truth.' He also works with scientists world over to bridge science and spirituality.

This book offers glimpses of Paramahamsa Nithyananda's journey towards Light. Through interesting incidents and great truths, it attempts to draw the reader to the profound experience behind the words. It is said that the life story of an enlightened master could bring forth a deep desire in an individual to evolve spiritually towards a better lifestyle, towards enlightenment itself. Read on for glimpses of a stirring life story of a great master on planet Earth.

To read about Nithyananda's biography in detail,
you may purchase a copy of the book
Paramahamsa Nithyananda Vol.1
which recounts His life up to the age of 17
The remaining volumes are yet to be published.

Taking birth

> "Every soul consciously decides the time, place, its parents and its mission, while taking birth on planet Earth."
>
> -Paramahamsa Nithyananda

It was under the glow of the spiritual magnet Arunachala and in the energy center reinforced by Arunachaleshwara that Paramahamsa Nithyananda was born as the second child of Arunachalam and Lokanayaki.

The Arunachala Hill is a spiritual incubator that has time and again given birth to enlightened Masters who have touched and transformed millions of seekers in the world. Just like how a clinical incubator preserves a baby, a spiritual incubator is needed to provide these enlightened beings with the right ambience when they take birth. Great Masters like Seshadri Swamigal, Bhagavan Sri Ramana Maharishi and Yogi Ramsuratkumar, to name a few, hail from Arunachala.

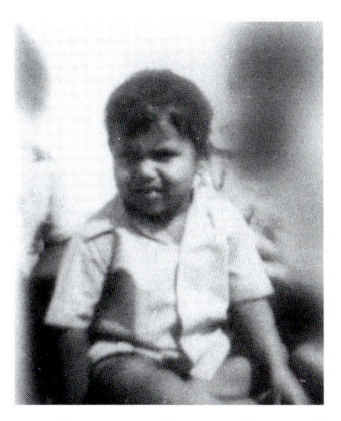

Paramahamsa nithyananda as a baby

Paramahamsa Nithyananda's mother discovered that she was pregnant with her second child when she was on a pilgrimage to the holy temple town of Tirupati in South India. On 1st January 1978, past midnight in the spiritual nerve center of Tiruvannamalai in South India, Paramahamsa Nithyananda was born. He was named Rajasekaran.

Today

Arunachala
- sacred hillock, manifestation of Shiva. Spiritual magnet that draws seekers from all over the world.

THE FAMILY PRIEST

> "My mission is not to prove my divinity. My mission is to prove your divinity."
>
> - Paramahamsa Nithyananda

> **Today**
>
> 'Don't come to me to predict your future. Come to me to design it! I am teaching you how to defy planetary influences, not how to tide over them!'
>
> - Paramahamsa Nithyananda

When the family priest drew up Paramahamsa Nithyananda's astrological horoscope, he found that the stars and planets had aligned themselves in an exceptional manner that he had seen for the first time. He declared to the startled parents that the baby would grow up to be a *raja sanyasi* - king amongst holy men. The priest considered himself blessed to have been able to cast the horoscope and stopped practicing astrology from then on.

YOGA AND WORSHIP

Raghupati Yogi, a friend and teacher

Paramahamsa Nithyananda's parents watched as mere guardians, without interfering, the spiritual growth in their child.

When Paramahamsa Nithyananda was about 3, he met Yogiraj Raghupati Maharaj. Raghupati Yogi was a yoga practitioner of great skills and powers. With a body as taut as a bowstring, disciplined by years of rigorous penance in India, Tibet and Burma, Raghupati Yogi was a friend and Guru to young Paramahamsa Nithyananda. With apparent foresight into the future, he prepared Paramahamsa Nithyananda's body through rigorous yogic training so it could hold the energy of enlightenment.

Raghupati Yogi

Parashakti
(Existential energy represented as a female form)
who appeared as a vision to Paramahamsa Nithyananda,
which he immediately carved out of soapstone as seen here.

"Yoga is union of man and God.
Worship is plain gratitude to Existence."

- Paramahamsa Nithyananda

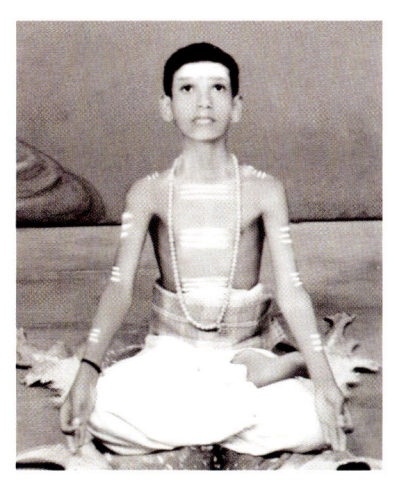

The earliest picture of Paramahamsa Nithyananda in meditation taken when he was 10 years old

Though Raghupati Yogi demonstrated to Paramahamsa Nithyananda, teleportation, levitation and other similar super normal feats, he also made him understand that these were not attributes of spiritual growth and that the understanding of the Supreme Truth lay beyond all this.

It was Raghupati Yogi who arranged for Paramahamsa Nithyananda to deliver his first public lecture on the *Patanjali Yoga Sutra* at the age of 10 in Tiruvannamalai. Distributing flyers for the occasion, he gathered over 1000 people for this unique event.

Today

Out of pure gratitude to Raghupati Yogi for the revolutionary training received, Paramahamsa Nithyananda has designed and offered to the world - Nithya Yoga, a yoga science and technique for enlightenment itself. Trained and dedicated Nithya Yogacharyas - teachers - carry this unique science to millions of people around the world.

ICONS AND WORSHIP

*"Worship is never 'of' the idol,
it is always 'through' the idol."*

- Paramahamsa Nithyananda

Paramahamsa Nithyananda ardently worshipped deities as live symbols of Existence, in his tiny altar at home. He carried this set of 5 deities with him wherever he went for worship.

Today

Nithyananda Sacred Arts Preservation is a special wing of Paramahamsa Nithyananda's mission that offers Indian Temple Heritage to humanity! Deities of stone, metal, wood and marble, temple structures in Dravidian style, sheet metal works, vehicles of Gods in wood, temple jewelry and costumes, puja offerings etc are created under the direct supervision of Paramahamsa Nithyananda. Skilled artisans from India dedicate their lives with endless gratitude to support this divine vision.

Puja items and parts of deity forms. Paramahamsa Nithyananda built deities with clay, decorated and worshipped them with great fervor and adoration. The temple town of Tiruvannamalai and the surrounding villages saw many festive creations of Paramahamsanithyananda and his friends

Ganesha eats...

Paramahamsa Nithyananda would offer food to this Ganesha deity everyday. He would plead and sometimes threaten the deity to eat the food he served him. One day, he heard a mythological story of a young boy who offered food to a deity that actually ate it. Determined to make his Ganesha eat the food that he served him, Paramahamsa Nithyananda resolved not to threaten him anymore. Instead *he* stopped eating until his Ganesha ate the food that was served by him.

Ganesha

At the end of the third day, the food disappeared! Overjoyed and feeling tremendous gratitude, he cried his heart out. He felt the power of devotion and faith strengthening further.

At the age of 12, Paramahamsa Nithyananda had a vision of a golden figure while at the altar of Goddess Parvati at the Arunachaleshwara temple. The vision made a deep impression on him. He took a copper sheet and with a nail etched it from memory.

Sri Chakra

The figure he drew was the sacred *Sri Chakra* believed to be a powerful and mystical representation of the Cosmos. When asked how he managed to carve with such ease this complex diagram that baffles even skilled artists today, Paramahamsa Nithyananda explained, 'It is just nine triangles placed at different angles to each other. Once you understand the concept it becomes easy!'

Today

In the temples created by Paramahamsa Nithyananda around the world, grand worship happens with the supreme understanding that worship is a wonderful spiritual technique to merge with Existence.

Pujacharya performing Sri Vidya Puja at the temple in the Los Angeles ashram

Vedanta and Tantra

> "Intellectual conviction strengthens the being, which is greater than mental and physical strengths."
> — Paramahamsa Nithyananda

Maataji Kuppammal - a catalytic force

Brahmayogini Vibhudhananda Devi Mataji Kuppammal was a spiritual guide and caretaker to Paramahamsa Nithyananda during his early days of spiritual growth in Arunachala. At the tender age of 12, when Paramahamsa Nithyananda was having deep spiritual experiences, Kuppammal took care of him physically and emotionally, explained to him his growing consciousness and trained him in various spiritual practices with an apparent foresight into the future.

Kuppammal & Paramahamsa Nithyananda

Isakki Swamigal, fostering spirituality

Isakki Swamigal, an enlightened master, was a main source of inspiration to young Paramahamsa Nithyananda. Fortunate to be with many enlightened masters, Paramahamsa Nithyananda grew up watching how ecstatic they were all the time. By seeing their brimming fulfillment and utter simplicity, his own yearning to attain, deepened.

Isakki Swamigal

Atma Purana (an Upanishad) a gift from Isakki Swamigal. This book marked the beginning of scriptural learning for Paramahamsa Nithyananda.

Atma Purana

Olai chuvadi

Olai chuvadi (palm-leaf manuscript) containing ancient vedic chants, which Paramahamsa Nithyananda received as a gift from Isakki Swamigal.

Today

At Paramahamsa Nithyananda's ashram, young brahmacharis and children of the gurukul chant vedic lore as part of the routine. Tuning to the divine intonations, the children grow up on a plane of elevated consciousness.

With Yogi Ramsuratkumar - a mystical bonding

Yogi Ramsuratkumar or Visiri Swamigal was an enlightened master, who was a contemporary of Bhagavan Sri Ramana Maharishi in Tiruvannamalai. He was well-known and well-liked in Tiruvannamalai. Paramahamsa Nithyananda became a regular visitor to this sage.

Yogi Ramsuratkumar would sit like a beggar amidst a pile of garbage that he collected on the steps of the building adjacent to *Thermutti*, where the temple chariot was parked. It was customary for people to stop by and ask him questions about their future. Children on their way to school would stop and ask how they would fare in their exams. They could rarely elicit a response from the intriguing mystic. One day, Paramahamsa Nithyananda stopped on his way to school and asked him if he would pass in his test in school that day. He got a reply, 'You will pass the test of life, my boy!'

Paramahamsa Nithyananda could not comprehend the meaning of those words at that time. A lady who sat nearby hearing this told him, 'Go on child! You will not understand these words now, but you will remember the truth of these words in time!'

At a festival graced by Yogi Ramsuratkumar in Tiruvannamalai

Annamalai Swamigal and the self inflicted wound

> "The courage to experiment with the Truth is the key to realizing it."
>
> - Paramahamsa Nithyananda

Annamalai Swamigal

Annamalai Swamigal was a direct disciple of Bhagavan Sri Ramana Maharishi. Around the age of 10, Paramahamsa Nithyananda started going to the Ramana ashram in Tiruvannamalai. He sat with Annamalai Swamigal's disciples regularly at the lecture sessions. One of the attractions of going to Annamalai Swamigal was that he used to distribute candies after his discourses!

One day, Annamalai Swamigal explained the concept of *maya* or illusion, when he said, 'We are not the body; this body is not real; what is real is the spirit; there is no pain that can affect this spirit; we are beyond pain and suffering.'

With these words ringing in his ears, Paramahamsa Nithyananda ran back home that day and taking a kitchen knife cut his right thigh to verify if he experienced pain. Intense pain resulted and scolding from his mother as well. He had multiple stitches from the doctor.

He went back to Annamalai Swamigal and demanded an explanation. Annamalai Swamigal said to him, 'The pain will go away. I will give you a technique to practice. Your very courage to experiment with the Truth will lead you to enlightenment.' This incident further deepened Paramahamsa Nithyananda's search.

Today

Paramahamsa Nithyananda is an inspiring personality to millions of people today! People gather to just be in the presence of a great Master...

Angkor Wat, Cambodia

GROWING CONSCIOUSNESS

"Meditation is the master key that can to open the door to your Self."

- Paramahamsa Nithyananda

Arunachala was Paramahamsa Nithyananda's everything. There was not a single crevice or rock that had not felt the fervor of his yearning. He could be perpetually seen meditating and basking in the glory of his beloved Arunachala. His structure was lean, but his eyes were always ablaze with an intensity that softened only upon seeing the inner Light. (Raghupati Yogi and Kuppammal were instrumental in shooting many pictures of him meditating, with apparent foresight.)

Today

Paramahamsa Nithyananda nurtures the meditator in every person through unique meditation programs. He creates the space in every individual to flower...

A Brush with Existence...

"As long as your hands are open,
you can feel the river flowing through it.
When you try to hold it, you miss it!"

— Paramahamsa Nithyananda

One day when he was about 12, Paramahamsa Nithyananda was sitting on a rock in the Arunachala hill and meditating; he was actually playing with the technique given to him by Annamalai Swamigal - to watch the source from where thoughts arose.

As he sat, slowly he felt himself dissolve. In his own words, 'Suddenly, I felt an opening in the inner space. Even with closed eyes I was able to see all 360 degrees! I felt the same life force not only inside my skin, but outside in other things also. I felt that I am alive in the rocks, in the plants, in the flowers in all the animate and inanimate things around me.

Paramahamsa Nithyananda meditating in Arunachala

Today

Brahmacharis of the Nithyananda Order perform holy bath to the sacred rock on the anniversary of Paramahamsa Nithyananda's spiritual experience

That was my first profound experience. It opened a deep compassion and love for everything. Great reverence for life happened through that experience. Acceptance of every being, as he is, entered my being, That experience was the first glimpse which happened in me which led to enlightenment. With just one such experience, one will see that all religious fanaticism, communal or linguistic fanaticism simply disappears from the system."

Paramahamsa Nithyananda's first spiritual experience was at sunset on *Buddha Purnima* day, the full moon day in the month of *Vaikasi* (May-June as per the Tamil calendar).

Primal fear on being attacked by Hyenas

Paramahamsa Nithyananda used to walk around the Arunachala mountain everyday. He would start very early in the morning, at around 4 am, and walk for three to four hours around the hill, chanting songs while walking. He was totally in the present, least bothered about what was going to happen the next moment - like an innocent child playing in the lap of his mother; an innocent child delighting in the ambience of his beloved Arunachala!

One morning he started very early, soon after midnight. In those days there was no road or lights on the path around the hill. It was just a jungle, a dense forest all the way. As he walked on, at a spot near a rivulet, a herd of hyenas approached him. He had been walking with his eyes cast downwards singing devotional songs. He was totally immersed in singing and did not notice the hyenas till he was very close to them. When he lifted his head and saw them, the animals were very close to him. From deep down his *hara*, from the *swadhishtana chakra* or spleen energy center point, he let out a loud scream. It was a scream of pure fear that he had experienced neither earlier nor after. Along with the scream he felt a total surrender to Arunachala and a deep trust that Arunachala would take care of him.

Suddenly, an elderly ascetic appeared in front of him from nowhere with a big stick and chased away the hyenas. As soon as the animals ran away, the old man disappeared. Paramahamsa Nithyananda did not know where this man came from nor where he went.

With that primal scream, Paramahamsa Nithyananda found that his body had suddenly turned much lighter; he started walking, almost floating as if the frequency of his being had increased.

(Primal therapy is a modern psychological treatment in which patients scream from deep down their hara, to relieve fear and other suppressed negative emotions in catharsis).

Schooling - A Mere Incident

> "Any work done with intensity
> becomes a meditation.
> Then life itself becomes meditative."
>
> - Paramahamsa Nithyananda

Schooling was a mere incident in Paramahamsa Nithyananda's life. At school, he wrote his record books at the chemistry and physics laboratories as a chore, but with more zest he chanted *mantras* and performed rituals.

Seen here are records that stand testimony to his fervor - a page from the mantra diary, a complete pictorial guide to doing *puja* (ritual deity worship) written by him. This book guides his disciples and public in *puja* practices today! His passion for ritual worship and the planning that came naturally with it at that tender age was amazing.

Paramahamsa Nithyananda's friends often teased him about his spiritual inclinations. One of them asked him what he was going to achieve with such long wasteful hours of meditation. He replied, 'When the time comes, you will know.'

Record notebooks and mantra diaries

Today

'When I was young, I yearned for a place where I could learn the secrets of blissful living under one roof. I searched for nine years but never found such a place. I had to pick it up in bits and pieces. After enlightenment, I wanted to first offer to the youth, such a place! The Gurukul and the Life Bliss Technology program are outcomes of this ardent desire. Here, the youth learn to explore and explode in infinite dimensions. They learn how to work without working, how to create blissful living through deep consciousness.

- Paramahamsa Nithyananda

- HIS NAME IS NITHYANANDA -

During a recent tour of Tamilnadu, after Paramahamsa Nithyananda had delivered a discourse and meditation in his hometown of Tiruvannamalai, he called his disciples to the stage of the packed hall and pointed to a few boys waiting in queue to take his blessings; these were the same ones who had questioned him earlier! They could be seen choking with emotion and shaking uncontrollably as they bowed down to touch the feet of the master. The disciples looked on, caught in their own emotions, as he took the boys in his arms with mischievous laughter and ardent compassion.

A diploma degree par excellence

Paramahamsa Nithyananda obtained a diploma in Mechanical Engineering at the Polytechnic in Gudiyatham, Tamilnadu. With just the attention he gave in classes, Paramahamsa Nithyananda breezed through his diploma course with flying colors. His teacher who taught him at college was his first initiated healer in his mission, just a few years later!

Cremation grounds of the holy town of Tiruvannamalai were serene places of meditation for Paramahamsa Nithyananda. He would return home only in the wee hours of the morning unlocking the house with the key given to him. His parents never uttered a word of disapproval at his unusual timings

Gurukul

Life Bliss Technology

17

In Search of Light

> "An ashram is an energy field
> where every path is a journey inwards."
>
> - Paramahamsa Nithyananda

Leaving home

The urge to leave home became stronger. One evening, the urge was so strong that Paramahamsa Nithyananda felt the need to act immediately. He felt he had to leave the life he was leading and enter into the life he was seeking without further delay. He could not bear to continue living the way he did any longer.

Paramahamsa Nithyananda wanted to tell his mother his decision first. He loved her deeply and wanted to make sure that her suffering was as little as possible. That night he went to his mother at around 10 pm and asked her, 'What will you do if I died?' His mother asked, 'Why do you ask me such an inauspicious question? What is wrong?' Paramahamsa Nithyananda said, 'Nothing, no particular reason, I just need to know.' His mother said resignedly, 'What can I do? I need to accept it if it happens.' He then told her that he wanted to leave home.

His mother burst into tears. Her body shook in sorrow uncontrollably. 'I knew that you would go away one day,' she said. He asked her whether she did not want him to leave. She said, 'No, I know that you want to go and I want you to do what you have always wanted to do in your life. I cannot stop you from that; but I cannot bear to see you go. That is why I am crying.'

Paramahamsa Nithyananda felt overwhelmed at the unconditional love of his mother. She was in deep sorrow and yet she wanted for her son what he wanted. She did not wish to be in his way. Her innocence and selfless love touched him deeply. She was innocent of her own innocence.

Across India and Nepal

Paramahamsa Nithyananda's deep yearning took him across India and Nepal, from Tapovan in the Himalayas to Kanyakumari in the South, and from Dwaraka in the West to Calcutta in the East. His *parivarajaka* (monastic wandering) lasted 9 years, preparing his whole being to experience the ultimate merger. Covering over 70,000 miles, many thousands of miles, he covered by foot.

"All great shrines are resonant with the Existential energy. Just being in them is a profound meditation."

- Paramahamsa Nithyananda

Mahavtar Babaji

Mahavtar Babaji is a living Himalayan Master. He gave darshan to Paramahamsa Nithyananda during his monastic wandering days in the Himalayas. It was Babaji who during this meeting called him as 'Paramahamsa Nithyananda', the name he is known by today!

Mahavtar Babaji

Today

Paramahamsa Nithyananda leads disciples to the Himalayan ranges and other high energy centers from time to time. Through the steps of spiritual wandering, he creates the space for the deep yearning in every being to fulfill.

Himalayan Trip 2007

*During his monastic wandering days, he would fill water in a water pot. He would first check the energy of the water by dangling this **rudraksh pendulum** over it and drink it only if the pendulum deemed it fit*

Saffron bag *for keeping holy ash, which traveled with him throughout his days of monastic wandering*

Rudraksh beads *from the string that he wore throughout his wandering days*

The first healing miracle

While returning from Tapovan, 17000 feet in the Himalayan range, Paramahamsa Nithyananda hitched a ride in an army truck. As the truck went over a ditch, he was thrown up and he landed on a metal piece that pierced and fractured his spine. The army doctor he was taken to wanted him to rest for 15 days. Paramahamsa Nithyananda paid no heed to him. Instead, he placed his own palm upon the injured area and moved on. When he was X-rayed at Haridwar everyone but him was stunned. The fracture had healed perfectly. Little did Paramahamsa Nithyananda realize that the healing touch upon his own body would one day benefit millions of people around the world!

Today

Healers initiated by Paramahamsa Nithyananda offer free Nithya Spiritual Healing service to the world at large

Manikarnika Ghat, Benares - the conquest of Death

This cremation area on the steps of the sacred river Ganga is considered to be the most sacred in Benares. It is said to be the point where Lord Shiva created the Universe.

Here, Paramahamsa Nithyananda had a conscious experience of death itself while in deep meditation. After the profound experience, he became aware that he had conquered the greatest and all pervading fear for every human being on planet Earth - the fear of death.

Manikarnika Ghat, Benares

Continuing his monastic wandering, Paramahamsa Nithyananda finally attained inner bliss at the age of 22. This is the first picture of him taken after his enlightenment. The fire in the eyes has gone; only supreme tranquility remains. Rajasekaran became Paramahamsa Nithyananda.

Today

Paramahamsa Nithyananda says, 'Spiritual wandering is a great technique and process for spiritual growth.' During the brahmacharyam training program, Paramahamsa Nithyananda sent out participants as wandering monks, to beg and receive alms! He said, 'Monastic begging is a technique to get detached from emotional fluctuations. When you beg for alms, you should be neither happy about what you get nor sad about what you miss!'

Early days of enlightenment

Guided by the invisible hand of Existence, Paramahamsa Nithyananda moved from Omkareshwar in Madhya Pradesh to Tamilnadu in the South of India, to a temporary abode on the banks of the river Kavery. Living on food brought by devotees and staying in the open or in huts, he performed many healing miracles. He conducted deity worships (*puja*), fire rituals (*homa*) and taught meditation in private and public gatherings, helping people with life solutions. News spread like wild fire about the young Swami with miraculous healing powers.

A Vision unfolds

"I have formulated a technology of bliss.
My mission is to make every individual realize that he is unique, infinite and that his true nature is bliss."

- Paramahamsa Nithyananda

Paramahamsa Nithyananda had already seen the land of his ashram in his vision - a sprawling area on the outskirts of Bangalore blessed with sacred signs: land of a 600 year old banyan tree, said to be the *jiva samadhi* (sacred burial spot) of an enlightened Master who had lived there for many years. The land was identified and Nithyananda Dhyanapeetam was formally inaugurated on
1 January 2003 at Bidadi, Bangalore on the day of his 26th birthday. In a celebration attended by spiritual and political leaders, it marked the beginning of a new saga in the history of planet Earth.

Today

Today, Paramahamsa Nithyananda is an inspiring personality for millions of people worldwide. From his experience of the Truth, he has formulated and gifted the *Technology of Bliss* to every individual.

His methods empower us to be physically and mentally fit individuals with sound spiritual strength. Millions of people around the world have experienced radical transformation through his techniques in short periods of time.

He gives the tools to live a creative and productive life guided by intuition and intelligence rather than by intellect or instinct. He shows the way to excellence in the outer world and radiance in the inner world both at the same time. His programs teach one to fall into the natural space known as meditation.

Paramahamsa Nithyananda says, 'Meditation is the master key that can bring success in the material world and deep fulfillment in your space within.' His powerful techniques and processes that comprise the meditation programs, help the flowering and explosion of individual consciousness in short periods of time.

Paramahamsa Nithyananda works with scientists and researchers world over to record the mystic phenomena through scientific data. He intrigues the world of medical science with results from his own neurological system. From the astounding observations, scientists feel that the potential for altering the rates and progression of diseases like heart ailments, cancer, arthritis, alcoholism etc. are beginning to look achievable.

Life Bliss Foundation is Paramahamsa Nithyananda's worldwide movement for meditation and transformation. Established in the year 2003 and now spanning over 1000 centers in 33 countries, the Life Bliss Foundation transforms humanity through transformation of the individual.

Nithyananda Meditation Academies (NMAs) worldwide serve as spiritual laboratories where inner growth is profound and outer growth is a natural consequence. These academies

Sacred Banyan tree, Bidadi ashram, India

are envisioned to be a place and space to explore and explode, through a host of activities, from meditation to science. They offer

Hyderabad ashram, India

quantum spirituality, where material and spiritual worlds merge and create blissful living; where creative intelligence stems from deep consciousness.

Many projects are in development at the various

Colombus ashram, Ohio, USA

academies worldwide; and new academies are being established to provide services in varied fields to humanity at large.

A diverse range of meditation programs and social services are offered worldwide through the Foundation. Free energy healing through the Nithya Spiritual Healing system, free education to youth, encouragement to art and culture, *satsangs* (spiritual circles), personality development programs, corporate programs, free medical camps and eye surgeries, free meals at all ashrams worldwide, a one-year residential spiritual training program in India, an in-house *gurukul* system of learning for children and many more services are offered around the world.

Ananda Sevaks of the Nithya Dheera Seva Sena (NDSS) volunteer force comprising growing numbers of dedicated volunteers around the world, support the mission with great enthusiasm.

Anandeshwara temple sanctum, Bidadi ashram

Salem ashram, India

Los Angeles ashram, USA

Contact us:

USA:

Nithyananda Dhyanapeetam
928 Huntington Dr,
Duarte,
Los Angeles
CA 91010
USA
Ph.: 1-626 205-3286
Email: Laashram@lifebliss.org
URL: www.lifebliss.org
       www.lifeblissgalleria.com
       shop@lifebliss.org

INDIA:

Nithyananda Dhyanapeetam
Nithyanandapuri
Kallugopahalli
Mysore Road, Bidadi
Bangalore - 562 109
Karnataka
INDIA
Ph.: 91 +80 65591844 / 27202084
Fax: 91 +80 27288207
Email: mail@dhyanapeetam.org
URL: www.dhyanapeetam.org

For other ashrams and centers worldwide, visit www.dhyanapeetam.org

Suggested for further reading...

Life Bliss Foundation offers many volumes of books and CDs across 23 languages. They are tools of blissful living for any type of person. A few of the books are listed here:

- Guaranteed Solutions for sex, fear, worry etc.
- Nithyananda Vol. 1 of Paramahamsa Nithyananda's biography
- Meditation is for you
- Bliss is the path and the goal
- The only way out is IN
- Rising in love with the Master
- Bhagavad Gita series
- 'Why' series
- A to Z 'click' books
- Uncommon answers to common questions
- Open the door...Let the breeze in!

To purchase books & other items

visit www.lifeblissgalleria.com
or contact us www.dhyanapeetam.org
www.lifebliss.org
www.nithyananda.org

❖❖❖ A vision that has come to be
A mission that is the master key
To take one from mind to no-mind
To bring bliss to all of mankind ❖❖❖